P9-BYO-758

A HISTORY MYSTERY™
THE DISAPPEARANCE OF THE ANASAZI

Other Baffling Mysteries in
A HISTORY MYSTERY *Series*
from Avon Camelot

THE CURSE OF THE HOPE DIAMOND
by Janet Hubbard-Brown

THE CURSE OF KING TUT'S TOMB
by Jay Montavon

THE MYSTERY OF THE ROSWELL UFO
by Ken McMurtry

THE SECRET OF ROANOKE ISLAND
by Janet Hubbard-Brown

WHAT HAPPENED TO AMELIA EARHART?
by Susan Landsman

WHO SHOT JFK?
by Susan Landsman

JANET HUBBARD-BROWN

Illustrated by Lino Saffioti

I am grateful to the following for their contributions to this book: Shannon Gilligan, Katharine Brown, Sammye Hubbard Vieh, Al Roth, Betty Howlett, Rick Rayfield, and Carol Wheelock.

A HISTORY MYSTERY: THE DISAPPEARANCE OF THE ANASAZI is an original publication of Avon Books. This work has never before appeared in book form.

AVON BOOKS
A division of
The Hearst Corporation
1350 Avenue of the Americas
New York, New York 10019

Cover photograph of Diorama #5 in Chapin Mesa Museum on Mesa Verde National Park in Colorado by Dale Anderson, Mesa Verde Museum Association, Inc.
Illustrations by Lino Saffioti
Published by arrangement with Whitbread Books
A History Mystery is a trademarked property of Shannon Gilligan/Whitbread Books.
Library of Congress Catalog Card Number: 92-22916
ISBN: 0-380-76845-3
RL: 5.7

Library of Congress Cataloging in Publication Data:
Hubbard-Brown, Janet.
The disappearance of the Anasazi / by Janet Hubbard-Brown ; illustrated by Lino Saffioti.
p. cm.—(A History mystery)
Includes bibliographical references.
Summary: Describes the discovery of Anasazi cliff dwellings in southwestern Colorado in 1874 and the speculations which arose about the origins and eventual fate of this Native American people.
1. Pueblo Indians—Juvenile literature. [1. Pueblo Indians. 2. Indians of North America.] I. Saffioti, Lino, ill. II. Title. III. Series.
E99.P9H825 1992 92-22916
978.9′01—dc20 CIP AC
First Avon Camelot Printing: December 1992

CAMELOT TRADEMARK REG. U.S. PAT. OFF. AND IN OTHER COUNTRIES, MARCA REGISTRADA, HECHO EN U.S.A.

Printed in the U.S.A.

OPM 10 9 8 7 6 5 4 3 2

Contents

Portrait of William Henry Jackson, date unknown.
(Courtesy of the National Parks Service, Scotts Bluff National Monument.)

Discovery!

William Henry Jackson stood on a cliff 700 feet above the ground at Mesa Verde in southwestern Colorado. (*Mesa verde* means "green table" in Spanish.) He was awestruck by the sight that greeted him. It was 1874. Jackson had climbed up to see if there really were houses tucked into the canyon walls. Someone had told him there were. He hadn't believed the stories until now. As he stared in wonder, his assistant's shouts coming from a few footholds below startled him.

"I don't know if I can make it!" the man named Ingersoll yelled up.

"You're almost here now!" Jackson reassured him. "You won't believe this. We've discovered a city!" Ingersoll pulled himself to the top, his face purple from the strain. He stopped and stared in disbelief at the cliff dwellings. "Will you look at this!" he exclaimed softly.

The others in their group had been defeated by the steep climb. Jackson and Ingersoll were alone in an Anasazi ruin that Jackson later named "Two-Story Cliff House." Though it was obvious the cliff houses were abandoned, as the two men walked around they felt the strong presence of others.

Jackson had been hired by the United States government to take pictures of mining activities in the Southwest. When a friend of his told him that he had heard there were cliff dwellings located up in the canyons, he decided to check it out.

Jackson headed toward the entrance. "Let's go in," he said to Ingersoll.

His assistant stood firm. "It wouldn't surprise me one bit if this place was haunted," he declared.

Jackson laughed. "Come on," he insisted. "You aren't scared of a few ghosts, are you?"

Ingersoll ignored the comment. He entered the building with Jackson, following closely behind him as they went from room to room.

Jackson stopped and picked up a pot, holding it up in the dim light. "This pot is beautiful," he declared. "These people were artists. But what I want to know is why they built their homes way up here. It's almost impossible to reach. It had to be for defense."

His companion gazed at the walls. "Look how this

place was made," he said admiringly. "These people had to get the stones, probably from the canyon slopes, then carry dirt and water to make the mortar, then fit the stones into the shape of the cave. How did they ever get those supporting timbers up here?"

The men also noticed that each stone block had been carefully chiseled into a particular shape.

It was starting to get dark. Jackson couldn't take any more pictures. "They must have had flying machines," Jackson laughed. "I've heard some of the Indians talking about it. No kidding. They say they've seen mysterious lights hovering over this area."

At that moment a gust of wind blew Ingersoll's hat off. It flew over the cliff and swirled downward until it was out of sight. Jackson didn't laugh this time. Without a word, both men walked to the path that would lead them back to civilization.

The Beginning

William Henry Jackson could not have known how close he was to describing the beliefs of many Native Americans of the Southwest. They say that supernatural beings, or ghosts, have been living in the Southwest since their legendary ancestors came up from beneath the earth. To these people, every butte, every canyon, cliff, and cloud has its own life and meaning. The landscape is filled with presences. They are not typical ghosts who form queer shapes in the fog or create eerie sounds. These invisible beings appear in silence, in air so clear and pure and still that objects which are known to be far away seem much closer. Jackson and his assistant noticed these spirits. Even today visitors speak of "eyes that are watching them."

The effect of such visits can be overwhelming. As a result, some people have devoted their lives to studying the Anasazi, trying to understand where these people came from and where they went after abandoning their highly developed civilizations.

But despite the years of study, we still don't even know their own name. "Anasazi" was bestowed on them by the Navajo years after their decline. *Anasazi*, literally translated from the Navajo language, Athapascan, means "the ancient enemies." However, *anaa* doesn't only mean enemy. It can also mean "strangers" or "other people" or "non-Navajo" or "illness." Most books and magazines choose to translate Anasazi into "ancient ones" or "the old ones."

The Anasazi had no written language. Some of their ruins have Spanish names because the Spanish invaded the Southwest in the sixteenth century. Others have English names that were given to them by people in the nineteenth and twentieth centuries who were discovering them for the first time. Names like Chaco Canyon, Mesa Verde, Canyon de Chelly, Betatakin, Cliff House, and Balcony House are but a few of the many ruins that have been excavated.

For people who do not even have a name of their own, the Anasazi and their descendants have left an enormous imprint on the area of the United States called the Southwest. Their belief systems, their lifeways, their gentle natures, and their relationship to the land have all seeped into the consciousness of the huge melting pot called the United States. People from all over the world come to see the ruins they

left behind. Many people also come to study the Anasazi's descendants, the modern Pueblo Indians of Arizona and New Mexico. When scientists created an orderly system by which to identify the different stages of the Anasazi, they called those who lived in the period after 700 A.D. Pueblo. *Pueblo* means "town" in Spanish.

The names of the Pueblo tribes are also the languages they speak. These languages go back 1,000 years. The Hopi are probably the best known of the descendants of the Anasazi because of the many books published containing their myths and prophecies. The word *hopi* means "peaceful ones," which creates a strong association in people's minds with the Anasazi, who are also believed to have been a gentle people. The Hopis and the Zuni are the westernmost Pueblos of today.

The other descendants of the Anasazi are the easternmost Pueblos—the Taos, Keresans, Tiwa, Tewa, and Towa. They live in the Rio Grande Valley now. They divide their people into moieties, or units, associated with summer and winter. The westernmost Pueblos are divided into clans that provide political and religious leadership. But all the Pueblo people share a common culture that was created by their ancestors, the Anasazi.

Who were the Anasazi? At the time Columbus arrived in America, the Anasazi world was thriving, active, and growing in the Southwest. In fact, just

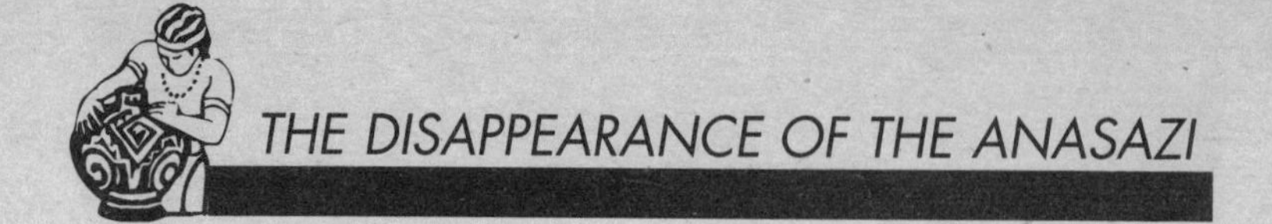

before the Spanish landed on the shores of what they believed to be a new world, there were approximately 40 million Native Americans living in the Western Hemisphere. Groups of gatherers and hunters, farming societies, and mighty empires were in existence here.

The area the Anasazi inhabited—the Four Corners area of the Southwest that includes Colorado, New Mexico, Utah, and Arizona—is one of the most beautiful landscapes on the continent. It continuously changes as the traveler journeys from Chaco Canyon in New Mexico to Mesa Verde in Colorado and on to Betatkin in Arizona. Chaco Canyon today probably isn't very different from the way it was 800 years ago. It is desert country. When driving on dirt roads through it there doesn't seem to be any escape from the withering hot sun. During the eleventh and twelfth centuries, the desert plain was dotted with more than five thousand Anasazi villages and as many as one hundred of them were large pueblos, or towns.

Then, like their neighbors, the ancient Mayans in Mexico to the south, the Anasazi seem to have vanished. Why would they abandon the communities it had taken them many years to create? Were they being attacked? There are no clearcut signs. Some people like to speculate that the Anasazi were brought to Earth from another planet and that they had to spend many years finding a way to return

This is a good example of a petroglyph that many people believe depicts a visitor from outer space. This in turn has given rise to theories that perhaps the Anasazi were taken away by such beings, or even descended from them.

(Courtesy of Chaco Culture National Historic Park, National Park Service.)

home. This could be based on an old Navajo story that says all the Anasazi gathered on a certain mesa and were whisked back to their own planet.

An opposite theory is that some outside force swept into the area and raised the Native Americans to a higher level of sophistication. That "outside force" could be extraterrestrial intervention, or intervention from other cultures.

There have been many UFO sightings reported in the Four Corners area of the Southwest. Dr. Diane Tessman is a UFO researcher and writer from Ireland. She doesn't doubt the connection between the Native Americans and UFOs. Native Americans practice an advanced form of mysticism and, Dr. Tessman points out, do not distinguish between nature on Earth and the cosmic energies out in space. White culture thinks of Earth and space as completely separate. Dr. Tessman wrote, "American Indians have lived as mystical beings for thousands of years and, in doing so, have encountered many other forms of life, from Earth and beyond."

On the other hand, if it wasn't extraterrestrial, did something more mundane like drought and starvation force the Anasazi to leave their astounding homes out in the desert and in the cliffs?

Some archaeologists look for clues to this leave-taking in the Anasazi beginnings. Over thousands of years the Anasazi developed a very sophisticated culture. They made tremendous achievements in the social, scientific, and technological fields. How did they learn to do all this?

There are different theories about where these people came from and when. Some of those theories are presented by experts who have studied the Anasazi for many years. Other theories are offered by people who are fascinated by ancient cultures. Versions of their origin have also been handed down from the Anasazi to their descendants—the modern-day Pueblos.

The purpose of any myth is to understand the unexplainable. Myths are the truth to people who

believe in them and live by them. They give guidance and spiritual strength. The well-known writer, Virginia Hamilton, wrote, "Lonely as they were, by themselves, early people looked inside themselves and expressed a longing to discover, to explain who they were, why they were, and from what and where they came." The myths of the Hopi and other Pueblo tribes can be very helpful in understanding the mystery of their ancestors, the Anasazi.

The most widely accepted theory among scientists is that the Anasazi came from Asia. It was certainly as long as 12,000 years ago. In a newspaper article published in the Washington Post in February of 1992, it was announced that scientists had found new evidence in a New Mexico cave that proved the human had entered the New World at least 28,000 years ago, and perhaps 38,000 years ago. That isn't so long ago when considering that the Earth is billions of years old, but it seems a very long time ago to those who are not used to thinking back further than 500 years, when Columbus sailed from Spain to America.

It took thousands of years for change to occur among the first Americans, called the Paleo-Indians. There were probably no major upheavals as they slowly made their way into the heart of the new country. It took many, many years for them to reach the Southwest. It was slow-motion migration.

When these ancient people came from Asia much

of the Earth was ice. It was as though the Earth was in the process of giving birth to North America as it exists today. The continent would swell and contract, creating huge lakes when the climate warmed and great glaciers when it cooled. All the ice made the level of the sea lower by as much as 300 feet. The Bering Strait which separates Siberia from Alaska became, during this Ice Age, a natural landbridge that the Paleo-Indians could walk across. It connected Asia and North America.

The immigrants had Mongoloid traits: copper-colored skin, dark eyes, straight black hair, and wide cheekbones. They had a full-size brain and a spoken language. They covered a territory over the years of more than 10,000 miles, from Alaska to Patagonia in South America. These people were hunters and gatherers who hunted animals much larger than they are today. They hunted mammoths and giant bison. They also hunted smaller animals such as rabbits, tapirs, llamas, and deer.

At the end of the Ice Age, the ancestors of the Anasazi found their way to the Southwest. There were other Indian cultures existing south of the Anasazi in Mesoamerica, the area that today covers Mexico and the countries in Central America. It is certain that the Mayans and other people living there directly influenced the Anasazi. There is a possibility that the Anasazi were also influenced by the Egyptians. That sounds farfetched, but there are many

who believe two civilizations—the Egyptians and the highly developed Mayan civilization of Mexico—were in contact. It is a fascinating theory, and one that many archaeologists don't agree with. A Norwegian explorer and ethnologist named Thor Heyerdahl believed there must have been one civilization that all the other ancient civilizations sprang up from. After all, he asks, how could sophisticated civilizations such as Mesopotamia, Egypt, and the Indus Valley all just happen to emerge about the same time: around 3000 B.C.? Heyerdahl has turned up evidence suggesting sea contacts among distant ancient cultures.

Other writers and explorers have offered the same theory. The artwork of the Egyptians and the Mesoamericans was similar, as were the myths and religious practices of ancient Egypt and Mexico. One writer figured that Egyptian contact occurred less than 1,500 years before the birth of Christ, maybe during the reign of Ramses III.

Heyerdahl goes as far as to speculate that the famed city of Atlantis perished in a flood. Could some of those people have escaped by boat, landing in different places such as the Nile, the Indus Valley, the Tigris and Euphrates—and, on the other side of the Atlantic Ocean, in the Gulf of Mexico? Did they try to recreate Atlantis in their new locations? Archaeologists shake their heads. Heyerdahl put his theory into action in 1947. He sailed the raft Kon-Tiki

Petroglyphs from Penasco Blanco. These drawings are actually carved into the rock rather than using color pigments. Animals were a frequent subject. So was the spiral design which is thought to represent both a shield used in war and the concept of the eternal flow of life.

(Courtesy of the Chaco Culture National Historic Park, National Park Service.)

across the Pacific Ocean to prove to scientists that crossing an ocean was possible in ancient times. An article entitled "Sailing Against the Current" in *U.S. News & World Report* (April 1, 1990) says, "Heyerdahl first roiled the quiet waters of academia by sailing the balsa log raft Kon-Tiki across the Pacific in 1947. Most scientists at the time dismissed, as they do now, the idea that such craft were capable of ocean-going trips and assumed the Pacific Islands were settled from Asia."

A Hopi myth says the Hopis originally came from the west, crossing the sea on boats or rafts from one "stepping-stone" or island to the next. Could the myth refer to their southern ancestors in Mexico or

South America who originally came from across the ocean? The ancient Mayas share the same myth. It is known that Uto-Aztecan populations in Mexico migrated to the Four Corners area long before the Anasazi built their extraordinary civilization.

One of the biggest questions in the world of archaeology arises. Does a civilization have to be influenced by another civilization in order to develop, or can a civilization develop on its own, willy-nilly? The solution to at least part of the Anasazi mystery rests in the answer to that question. Did the Anasazi have any help developing their large society? The writer Scott Peterson warns that it is racist to believe that the Native Americans were incapable of such huge advances in civilization. Is the theory held by the majority of scientists true, that humans arose more or less at the same time in many parts of the world? No one knows the answer.

The climate in the Southwest, today so hot and arid, was wetter and cooler when the hunters came. There were enormous grasslands. Trees and reeds grew alongside the many streams. The people came to have a close relationship with the land which fed them and gave them shelter. They learned where to find water, firewood, stone for making tools, game to kill and eat, and shelter.

In time, the great desert of the Southwest began to form. The bison became extinct and the buffalo became the most hunted animal. The people also de-

pended on wild plant foods. They wove baskets and began storing food, mostly seeds and nuts, which meant they had to return to where the food was stored. They began staying closer to home. And when corn entered their lives by about 1000 B.C., everything changed.

Corn had been domesticated in Mexico by around 4000 B.C. from a wild grass that grew in the tropics. At first only small ears were produced. The Native Americans probably dropped a few seeds into the ground, then went on their hunting journeys. When they came back, they found that at least some of the seeds had taken root. But it took a long time for them to come to rely on corn as a main food source. Archaeologists begin calling the Anasazi their Navajo name when farming became more important than hunting and gathering. This happened after 100 A.D. At the same time, pottery discovered at these earliest sites seems to have come from Mexico.

Three cultures developed in different parts of the Southwest in late prehistoric times: the Mogollon, the Hohokam, and the Anasazi. All three cultures traded corn and pottery and various technologies. All were learning how to farm with very little water. There were also other cultures such as the Sinagua who lived around present-day Flagstaff, Arizona, and the Salado who farmed the upper Salt River Valley.

The Mogollon peoples are best known for their

An excellent example of the famed black on white Anasazi pottery, from Chaco Canyon.

(Courtesy of Chaco Culture National Historic Park, National Park Service.)

spectacular pottery, even though in time all tribes were famous for their pottery. All Mogollon culture disappeared around 1250, except Casa Grandes, which survived into the fifteenth century.

The word *hohokam*, loosely translated, means "the vanished ones." The Hohokam lived in the Sonoran Desert. Some experts believe they migrated from Mexico into Arizona around 300 B.C. There is no question that they maintained active ties with Mexican peoples. The Hohokam were known for their water systems, which the Anasazi later adopted. No more than 125 houses existed in their locale, Snaketown, at any one time. Hohokam culture died out around 1450.

The Anasazi went much further in developing a civilization, becoming known for their building

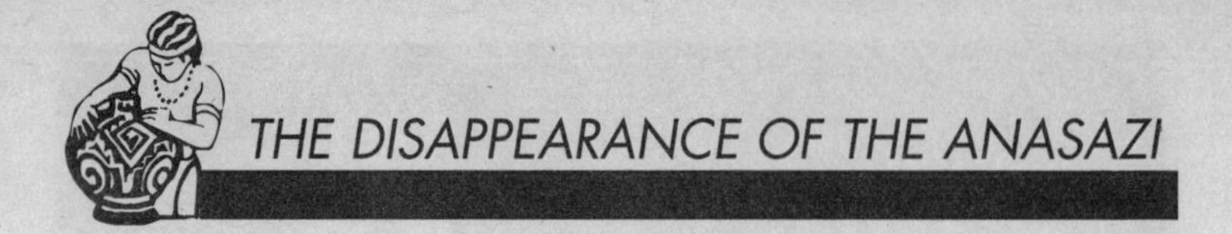

styles, their innovative farming techniques, and their ability to adapt. They settled in a land of majestic mesas, canyons, and open sagebrush country. The early people were labeled the "Basketmakers" by archaeologists because of the many varieties of baskets found at the Anasazi ruins, some so tightly woven they could hold water. Their houses were named "pithouses" by the archaeologists who discovered them because they were dug into the ground. In a later phase, the Anasazi began to gather in larger settlements both at high elevations and in the canyons. They built storage areas on the surface, above the ground.

More and more people moved into the Four Corners region during the years between 900 A.D. and 1200. Today we would say there was a "population explosion" and what followed was a "building boom." An operation like the one that existed at Chaco Canyon had to be organized.

The most well-known of the Chacoan ruins are located on a strip of land about ten miles long. There are many multi-storied towns located in the area and outside the towns are smaller village sites. They are one story high and have an average of sixteen rooms.

The largest town is Pueblo Bonito, which means "beautiful village." It has more than 600 rooms. It is a D-shaped building, covers nearly three acres and is four or five stories high in places. Perhaps as many as a thousand people lived there. The Anasazi used

An aerial view of Pueblo Bonito. As many as a thousand people lived there at once. Parts of it were once five stories high!

(Courtesy of Chaco Culture National Historic Park, National Park Service.)

materials from the earth to build their towns. The places they built seem to blend into the landscape. The people who developed roads and built gigantic stone structures were engineers and craftsmen of the highest order. Huge trade networks developed. Pottery skills flourished.

Then, just as the most fantastic culture developed in the Americas to that time was reaching its zenith, it all stopped. The people left. Where did they go? And why? And who cared? No one did for a long time until the day that William Jackson discovered the cliff dwellings at Mesa Verde in 1874.

Digging into the Past

The answer to Jackson's questions about the fate of the Anasazi lies in their ruins. The study of ruins is called archaeology. But, when William Jackson climbed up to Two-Story Cliff House in 1874, archaeology wasn't yet considered a real science.

Thomas Jefferson, the author of the Declaration of Independence, is often referred to as the father of archaeology. During the time he lived, Americans were discovering large mounds all over the country which could not be easily explained. Thousands of these mounds were located throughout eastern America between the Appalachians and the Mississippi River. Jefferson, who lived in Virginia, concentrated on the mounds in his part of the country when he was researching them. Jefferson described his excavation of prehistoric Indian mounds in 1781. He wrote down all he observed and drew conclusions

from his observations. He began to understand that the artifacts were found in layers, each indicating a distinct period in time. And last, he came to a conclusion about the Native Americans' origin. He was of the same mind as the archaeologists of today who believe the Native Americans originally crossed the Bering Strait into America.

Strangely enough, his report was ignored for decades. It was too factual for the new immigrants who preferred to make great stories out of all the different theories that arose about the mounds. One theory was that the American Indians were descended from the Jews. William Penn, the founder of Pennsylvania, said the Indians reminded him of Jews he had seen in London. Benjamin Franklin thought the mounds were built by the Spanish explorer Hernando de Soto.

No one wanted to admit the Indians who they considered ignorant, lazy savages could have built the mounds. A governor of New York thought the mounds in that state had been raised by Vikings. A postmaster in Ohio wrote that the mounds there had been built by Hindu immigrants from India. Once the new Americans had convinced themselves that a more noble race than the Indians had constructed the impressive mounds, they theorized that those same noble people vanished under terrible circumstances. A favorite notion was that some barbarians had come in and killed them.

One man, James H. McCulloh, Jr., compared a small number of ancient skeletons from the mounds with those of living Native Americans in 1829 and concluded they were of the same race. Eventually, inspired by Jefferson, various societies were formed to try to present the whole truth.

The Smithsonian Institution was one of those societies. Founded by James Smithson, an amateur scientist, the purpose of the Institution was "to found an establishment for the increase and diffusion of knowledge among men." The Institution's first publications were on the mounds and American prehistory. As time went on, more and more attention was focused on archaeological research.

Wonderful new discoveries were made during the last decades of the nineteenth century, including Jackson's discovery of the Anasazi ruins in the Southwest. Even so, it took Americans a long time to realize that the ruins of the Anasazi and other Native Americans are as much a part of their American heritage as the White House.

During this period, an ethnographer named Frank Hamilton Cushing, long fascinated by the Native Americans, joined an expedition to the Southwest. He was taken in by the Zuni of the modern-day Pueblos and soon adopted their dress and diet and learned their language. He stayed with the Zuni for five years. This was the first example of someone totally immersing himself in a project in this way. Cushing

Cliff dwellings at Mesa Verde in Colorado. Villages such as these were built next to the cliff for protection from weather and intruders.

(Courtesy of the National Museum of The American Indian, Smithsonian Institution.)

connected the pots and stones he saw in use in the nineteenth century with the ones he excavated from earlier periods. That hadn't been done before. It was a radical approach. Today, archaeologists and anthropologists do much the same thing to try to understand the vanished Anasazi. Scientists study the Anasazi's descendants in today's pueblos looking for clues to these people of the past.

The job of the archaeologist is to record everything uncovered at an excavation. Specific objects and the layers of earth in which they were found are important to note. It is almost impossible to date an object that is seen in a museum. However, if an object, such as a spear, is found in the skeleton of a certain species of bison buried beneath many layers of soil, then the scientist can safely say that it is 10,000 years old. Why? Because that species—the bison—became extinct then.

Imagine being an archaeologist in the year 9000, more than 7000 years from now. You are living on a pollution-free planet and are going to Planet Earth to check out the ruins of a city called New York. The skyscrapers would inspire awe. One main street in Manhattan is referred to as "Tombstone Alley" because all the skyscrapers lined up there look like giant tombstones. Perhaps the archaeologists of the distant future would think of these buildings the way we think about pyramids. Perhaps they would speculate that the people who lived so long ago must have been trying to build to a bridge heaven.

Imagine the types of artifacts they would find: computers, yellow taxi cabs, televisions, waterbeds, high heel shoes, cookware, dishes, milk cartons, Ben and Jerry's ice cream containers, and Nintendo machines. Of course there would be books—millions of them, no doubt.

Paintings at the Metropolitan Museum and the Museum of Modern Art would be studied for clues leading to how New Yorkers responded to life. Perhaps some of the walls of St. Patrick's Cathedral would still be standing. The archaeologists would dig through all the rubble and find icons of the Virgin

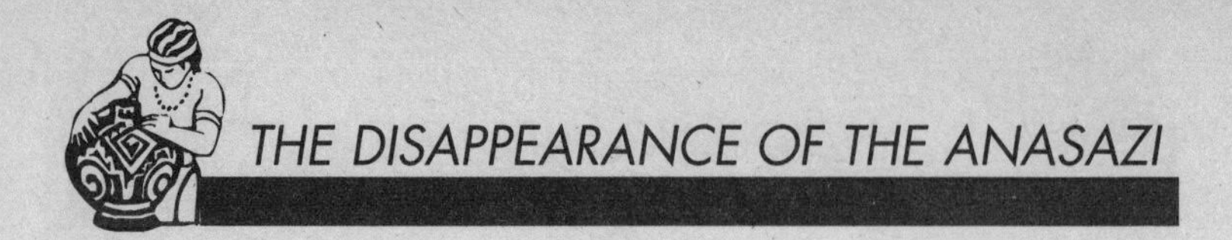

Mary and Jesus. They would enter a Jewish home and trace a painting there back to Eastern Europe or enter Sardi's Restaurant and understand from all the caricatures on the walls of theater personalities that theater was important.

They would no doubt be amazed at all the different kinds of people who lived together in one place. But it wouldn't take them long to realize these people were not one happy clan. The future archaeologists would find a body riddled with bullet holes which might lead them to believe there were enemies from the outside. Other skeletons would be laid out in wooden boxes wearing makeup and their Sunday best. Would that indicate they believed in life after death?

And the trash! Archaeologists rely heavily on discards. What would the mountains of crushed garbage and trash tell them?

What would they think of the Statue of Liberty? Would they believe her to be the great Goddess of the Sea?

It isn't uncommon for a scientist to spend an entire lifetime studying and analyzing the layers upon layers of secrets buried in the ruins. This process requires the same perseverance demanded of a detective on the trail of a murderer. Every handprint, every trinket found, every bit of skeleton adds an-

There are still many Anasazi sites to be studied. Here are some archeologists at work at the Sand Canyon Pueblo near Cortez, Colorado. (Rick Bell, Crow Canyon Archeological Center).

other piece to an enormous and never–ending jigsaw puzzle.

Most of these scientists spend a lot of time at digs, particularly during the summer months. They spend hours each day mapping out the ruin, carefully digging through the dirt seeking clues. Is a miniature stick–doll a toy or a religious object? This is the kind of question archeologists and anthropologists ask and then try to answer. All the information gets fed into a computer. They also use computers to scan topographic maps to identify possible locations for ruins.

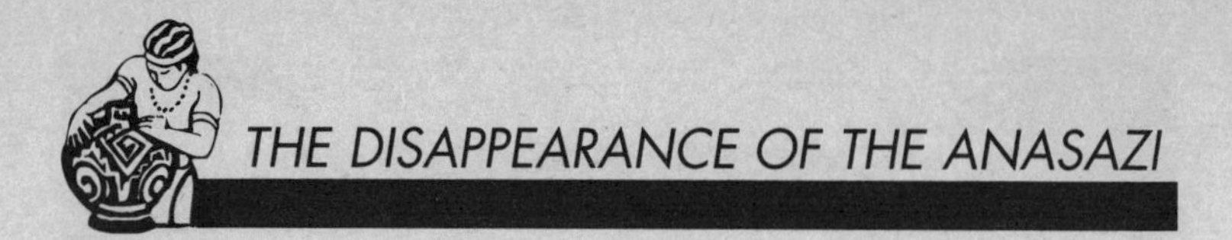

Trash heaps around ruins are treasure troves for the archaeologists. Broken pottery, old clothing, animal bones, dirt, and broken tools all offer major clues. Trash can tell a trained observer a great deal about a culture. Anasazi refuse dumps are called middens. They are considered sacred, because Native Americans believe that all things from the earth must be returned to the earth. They were often used as burial grounds by the Anasazi.

Pottery is one of the main ways these scientists have of understanding the Anasazi. Potsherds, which are the jagged fragments of broken pots, are pieced together to make a pot. Nearly everyone in an ancient culture tended to make pottery of the same general style. Sometimes scientists can match the clay in the pottery to the exact location where it is from. They can also date the pottery to within fifty years of when it was made, as pottery decoration changed with nearly every generation.

A certain type of pottery bowl has been found in burial sites. Almost all of these bowls have had a hole punched into them. Scientists believe this was done at the burial to release the spirit of the bowl so that it could go with the dead person on his journey to the next world. This tradition was one of many that the Anasazi learned from the Mayas.

When bones and remains of plant life are found in the middens, scientists ran date layers in the mounds much more easily. Radiocarbon dating is a

common procedure. It measures the decay of carbon 14, an element present in all living organisms. And the bones of dead animals are X-rayed to determine how the animal died. These two scientific methods greatly advanced what scientists could learn about these ancient cultures.

Another method of dating ruins and events was developed by Dr. Andrew E. Douglass in the early 1900s. Tree-ring dating helps archaeologists to tell when trees were cut and to determine the amount of moisture in a given year. Every year living trees produce a new growth ring. Douglass learned to identify distinctive patterns of a tree's growth as preserved in its rings. From that, an analyst can figure out when the tree lived, and even the year it was cut for a roof beam.

Mistakes in the field of archaeology can occur. In the 1930s, a strong-willed anthropologist with the Smithsonian Institution decided that Asians could not have come to this continent until after the Ice Age and whenever anyone would dispute this, he would write damaging attacks against the critic. To avoid arguments, no one approached the subject for years.

Another more amusing example was when the head shapes of the Anasazi changed. This phenomenon convinced archaeologists that a different culture had entered the realm of the Anasazi around 700 A.D. and taken over. But the answer was much more simple than that. Mothers had begun putting their babies in portable cradles made with hard boards. The boards pressed against the backs of the babies' soft skulls, which flattened the rear of the head. The sides of the skull bulged out. This practice changed the head shape of an entire people!

The naming of Anasazi sites and time periods began to cause confusion as more scientists studied the Anasazi. So many archaeologists in different parts of the United States were giving different names to the time periods of the Anasazi that there was much confusion. A national conference was held in 1927 which was the first cooperative effort to agree on the names and time periods.

The trained archaeologists still have to contend with the sensationalists, those who want to build good stories rather than accept the facts. And people haven't changed. They are more likely to pay attention to some farfetched story about the vanished Anasazi and other cultures than they are to straight facts that point to a solution as simple as bad weather forcing those people to move.

On the other hand, it isn't uncommon for the scientific community to turn up their noses at people who take unusual approaches. Thor Heyerdahl is not readily accepted among archaeologists, even though he has spent his life proving his theory that there could be an Egyptian/Mesoamerican connection.

Flights of imagination are often unacceptable to the scientific world.

The imagination opens these people and this land to us. Linda Cordell, an expert on the Southwest ruins, wrote, "There are always times of silence, solitude, and peace in the open and quite empty land of the Southwest. There are treasured moments spent alone pondering the low mounds of tumbled walls or gazing at an ancient image engraved in stone. At those times one feels a spiritual communion with the past and with the land."

And what do the Native Americans have to say about all this? Alfonso Ortiz is a scholar and writer of the Tewa community. He wrote, "A Tewa is not so interested in the work of archaeologists. A Tewa is interested in our own story of our origin, for it holds all that we need to know about our people, and how one should live as a human. The story defines our society. It tells me who I am, where I came from, the boundaries of my world, what kind of order exists within it; how suffering, evil, and death came into this world; and what is likely to happen to me when I die." There is much more mystery around the Anasazi than just their disappearance.

Cheto Ketl, the Great Kiva at Chaco Canyon. Only a few of the Great Kivas were ever built. Why so few existed remains a mystery.

(Courtesy of Chaco Culture National Historic Park, National Park Service.)

Mysteries Within and Without

Hopi legend says that the ancestors of the Anasazi emerged into this world from an earlier home somewhere below the surface of the earth. They came up through the "navel of the world," which is what the hole in the floor found in all kivas represents. *Kiva* means "world below." The hole is called a *sipapu*. Great mystery lurks in the underground structures called kivas found in all the Anasazi ruins, just as mystery fills the cathedrals in Europe built in the Middle Ages.

The kiva is where rituals and special ceremonies were performed, and still are today. No village, no matter how small, was complete without a kiva. They have changed size, shape, and purpose over

Ruins of the Anasazi village of Pueblo Bonito at Chaco Canyon. The round rooms were probably used for religious purposes. Today the area is part of a national park.
(Courtesy of Chaco Culture National Historic Park, National Park Service.)

many years. They developed out of the first houses the Anasazi ever built, the pithouses. Pithouses were small and dug into the ground about eighteen to twenty-four inches and if necessary, retaining walls were built up around the usually circular structure. They had central firepits. The roof entryway acted as a smokehole. A ventilator shaft from the outside was connected to a tunnel that entered at or under floor level.

Pithouses were practical because, as long as the floor of the pithouse was lower than the level where the ground froze, the temperature in the house would not drop below freezing. The underground structures were probably cooler in the summer. The upper walls and roof were made out of wood and dried mud. Some used ladders to enter their under-

ground homes; the more shallow pithouses had an opening on the southeast side of the house. Inside there was a hearth.

As the Anasazi began to build their homes above the surface of the earth after 900 A.D., the pithouses began to serve as "club houses" for the men and ceremonial rooms for all. Archaeologists began calling the circular structures kivas. In the floor archaeologists often find a sipapu, which acted as a communication link to the spirit world. Here is where the men wove cotton and told their stories. Here is where rituals and ceremonies were enacted. Men drummed while dancers called forth the energy from the earth. Healings took place in the underground chambers. Later, the kiva was the only safe place where the Pueblo tribes could hide from white invaders. Outsiders, even to this day, are not allowed in.

A writer described what it felt like to enter a kiva at one of the ruins called Bandelier, "You truly feel reborn when you rise from this stone womb into an almost perfect hemisphere of sky, mountain, pine and rock."

The Pueblo today use a ladder for entering and exiting the kiva. In some kivas, the end is widened and forms the same shape as the T-shaped doorways in all the ancient Anasazi ruins. Archaeologists theorize that the T-shaped doors have religious significance. One such theory is that the shape made it easier for the spirits to leave. Ceremonial objects have been found in kivas that go back as far as the earliest farming Anasazi. (100 B.C., to 500 or 700 A.D.) There are human-shaped clay figurines, corn-cobs decorated with sticks or feathers; polished stone disks; a "medicine bag" containing small objects, and tapered stone cylinders probably used as tobacco pipes.

The pictographs and petroglyphs found in kivas and on rocks all across the Southwest were a part of the religion. Native Americans didn't see any difference between religion and art and everyday activities. Some people have speculated that rock art comprised both writings and maps of the prehistoric Americans, but most experts agree the drawings are related to religious activities. Some are believed to portray supernatural ideas. There are many geometric figures, hunting scenes, and possibly mythical beings. A number of researchers have used the drawings to prove that extraterrestrial beings had been in the area. Many figures look uncannily like astronauts of today. And images that resemble current popular images of spaceships are eerie.

Ceremonies, in Anasazi times as well as today, are held on the roofs of the kivas in the villages, which often serve as plazas. Their religion is of the earth. Author Erna Fergusson wrote, "I thought of all these brown people whom I had seen dancing their prayers, pounding them with their feet into the earth, which is their mother. Her ways are close to

Pictographs created by actual hands dipped in a dark red pigment. The significance of the images are not fully understood.

(Courtesy of Chaco Culture National Historic Park, National Park Service.)

them, even when they are hurt. They understand the earth, they dance their prayers into the earth, and they pray for real things—for sun, and rain and corn—for growth, for life."

For most Native Americans, all life is one. Their religion could be called nature mysticism. Mayan ideas strongly influenced the Native Americans of North America. The Mayan understanding of the sacredness of all creation is the foundation upon which Native American thought is built. The Great Spirit, or Creator, created all things and is reflected in all things. A tree, an animal, or the stars are as worthy of honor as a human being.

To a Hopi, for example, the world where he or she lives is the human world and in it all the animals,

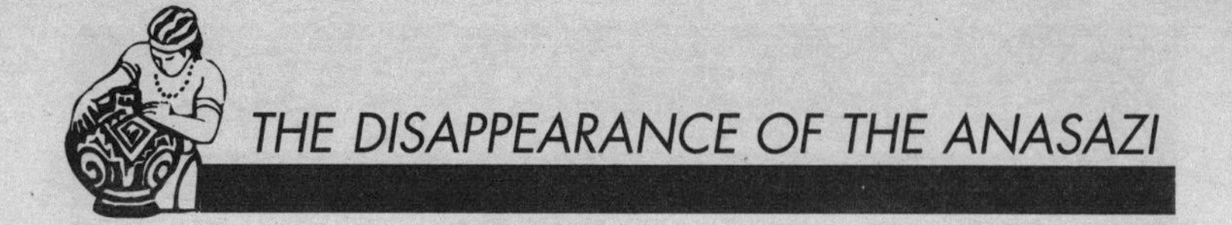

birds, and insects appear in disguise. But these creatures who share the spark of life with humans must have other homes where they live in human forms like ourselves. They are thought of as human. Prayer offerings are sent forth for the kind of game animal the hunter is going to hunt. Forgiveness is begged of the animal or plant about to be killed.

Along with the hundreds of average-size kivas that were so common in Anasazi villages were the Great Kivas that must have served many more people at a time, much as our churches do today. Eight have been excavated in Chaco Canyon and others have been found scattered throughout the Four Corners area. As their name implies, they are much larger than the average kivas. Some are fifty or more feet in diameter. One photographed at Pueblo Bonito reminds one of a Roman coliseum.

Some scientists think that these awesome structures indicate a priesthood that would have been similar to a ruling class. It would have taken tremendous organization and authority from some group to direct the tremendous labor force that was necessary to build the Great Kivas. Everything leading up to the Great Kivas however, has pointed to an extremely democratic people who would have shunned such authority in their lives. And yet, the buildings that obviously were used for ceremonies that included large numbers of people were significant.

The mysterious, almost sinister Anasazi Tri-Wall structures have a Mexican influence, too. They were large three-walled buildings, each designed like a maze. Were they religious centers? There are only a few of these structures remaining. One is at Pueblo del Arrajo at Chaco Canyon and two are at Mesa Verde. Some people believe these walls were the temples of a Mexican god who was worshiped through much of Mexico and Central America. Could they be the residences of the newly developed priest class? Or might they have been put in certain places to call forth water?

That brings another mystery. Is it possible that the Anasazi understood geomancy? The earth's surface is a huge field of energy.

In imperial China, the geomancers (diviners of the earth) were responsible for maintaining the flow of spiritual energies throughout the land. By doing so, harmony and prosperity flowed in the countryside. Positioning of roads and buildings in relation to the earth energies was probably studied by the Anasazi, as it was on other continents in ancient times. Egyptian temples are but one example of how buildings were positioned at certain angles in order to exist in harmony with the rising and setting of the heavenly bodies at particular times of the year.

The Hopis who now live on three gigantic mesas in the Southwest are certain that their ancestors were guided to where they are today. That knowledge is based on their psychic intuition. But what about the scientific view? Think of the earth as a great gyroscope forever spinning at a fixed angle. This is caused by convection currents set in motion by radioactivity in the middle of the earth. Many scientists agree that our present continents have broken away from greater land masses. With continental drifts there are different directions at different times for north. Magnetic north was once in the middle of the Pacific Ocean and then in the Southwest where the Hopis live today. The Hopis didn't try to figure out scientifically that their current home was the polar center of the earth when they moved there. They just knew.

Like the present-day Hopis, the Anasazi watched sunrise and sunset every day, noting the point on the horizon where the sun first peeked over the canyon rim. The position of sunrise and sunset on the horizon changes a little from day to day, coming to a stop at the summer and winter solstices. It then reverses. This change told the people when to plant their crops and hold celebrations. The position of the sun on the horizon was important for directions, a calendar, and religious reasons.

The inhabitants of Chaco Canyon created a solar observatory. They invented the "sun dagger" clock, a seasonal clock whereby the seasons strike on a clock of stone. Spiral patterns, carved into natural rock, caught shafts of light between other rocks at solstice

A dagger of light strikes a stone, signifying the summer solstice. Note the carved spirals on the rock, almost making a clock face. At Fajada Butte in Chaco Canyon.

(Courtesy of Chaco Culture National Historic Park, National Park Service.)

time and equinox time. In some villages, observations were made from indoors through special windows.

A similar practice was occurring during the Stone Age in England at different megaliths. The most famous is Stonehenge. And there is a cell at Xochicalco in Mexico where a sunbeam enters through the roof and forms a narrow streak of light at noon on the summer solstice.

Is it coincidence that people in different parts of the world were creating seasonal clocks? People who study such phenomena are called astro-archaeologists. They combine the study of astronomy and archaeology.

As archaeologists began digging in the ruins of Mesa Verde, Chaco Canyon, and other Anasazi sites, they uncovered more mysteries. A road system was discovered that puzzled everyone. The Anasazi didn't have wheels or animals to haul supplies. Why did they need roads? One archaeologist has identified nearly 500 miles of possible roads. Five major roads come together at Pueblo Alto at Chaco Canyon. At one point, the road swells to four separate lanes, wider than any of today's interstate highways. They were straight. If a mesa was in the way they simply carved footsteps into it. No one really knows why they were built. They do know that such an undertaking required a huge labor force. Some of the practical possibilities are that they were used for ceremonial processions, to move large numbers of workers between towns, for communications, and for trade.

Lights on mesa tops were part of a communication system that carried messages to distant points. One school of thought holds that these sites were located so that fires, or sunlight reflected by mica mirrors, could be seen for great distances between the outlying districts.

Their water control systems were an amazing feat, too. At Mesa Verde they built stone-check dams near streams. They trapped soil and slowed the runoff of

A view of the "Sun Dagger" slipping past the carefully aligned stones. Since the Anasazi were intimately in tune with nature, the purpose of the clock was less agricultural and more religious.

(Courtesy of Chaco Culture National Historic Park, National Park Service.)

rain and snowmelt. They also built a reservoir, and the water contained was a source of drinking water for several communities built around it. At Chaco Canyon, they did flood farming as there were no streams that ran steadily. They built dams to collect run-off water from the canyons, then constructed dikes that diverted the water up the canyon into the fields.

How strong was the Mexican influence on the Anasazi? The greatest evidence is found at Chaco Canyon. The excavation of Pueblo Bonito revealed shell and turquoise, parrot feathers and copper bells (originating in Mexico), and pottery which originated far to the south and southwest. The religious influence seems greater than archaeologists thought at first, particularly at Chaco Canyon. Pueblo Bonito, is the largest pueblo, or town, in Chaco Canyon. It has over 600 rooms and is five stories high. It contains as many as a million dressed stones. The masonry work is outstanding, the best in the Southwest. Where did the Anasazi learn how to build like that? Frank Lee Earley, writing about Chaco Canyon in 1976, refers to two groups of people living there before the city was abandoned: the early Bonitians and the late Bonitians who arrived in the early 1000s. His theory is that the late Bonitians moved in and took over. Where did they come from? Did they come from Mexico? They had to have been the master builders. Earley believes the early Bonitians did not

mingle with the newcomers. And why were the late Bonitians the first to leave? Was it they who were responsible for the exodus out of Chaco Canyon? The warlike Aztecs were overpowering the Toltec civilization in Mexico at this time. Were Aztecs creating trouble for the Anasazi, too?

Many scientists have determined that the ancient city of Pueblo Bonito served as an immense distribution point. With so many people living in the city and the outlying districts, there would have to have been a central location. Others see the large towns serving as ceremonial centers where people came from many miles away to visit.

The reason archaeologists think Pueblo Bonito was not inhabited by as many people as originally thought is they can't find enough bodies. Where did these people bury their dead? They generally didn't believe in cremation. This lack of remains of the dead occurs in other ruins, too. Where are the bodies?

From the discovered graves, it becomes apparent that the Anasazi believed in some existence after this one. Found in nearly every burial is a pair of new, unworn sandals. Also found in graves were food, weapons, baskets, nets, beads, ornaments, digging-sticks, and stone pipes. It isn't uncommon to find group burials as well.

The burial pits were lined with bark, grass, or fiber and the bodies covered with the same materials. Slabs of stone, poles, brush, and dirt were laid down as covers for the tombs. The bodies have at times been referred to as mummies, but that is an incorrect term for them because they were not preserved chemically. The exceptionally dry climate preserved them naturally.

In one major ruin, for example, seven burials have been found that covered more than one hundred years of occupation. And those bodies were those of children or young females. Where are the males?

Some strange remains have been uncovered. A man wearing leather moccasins was found in an Arizona pit. Moccasins were a rare item among the Anasazi. His body had been cut in two at the waist, apparently after death, and then sewn together again. Was he a stranger from a faraway tribe who had met death in Anasazi country?

Another pit in northeastern Arizona contained only a pair of arms and hands, lying palms-up on a bed of grass. Three handsome necklaces of abalone shell were wrapped around the wrists, and two pairs of magnificent sandals were included in the grave offerings. A large basket was placed over the remains. Was this the last resting place of someone who had met a terrible death?

There is some evidence of cannibalism at a number of sites during the later periods, but not enough study has been done to figure out how widespread it was. Many burned dwellings and human skeletons that had been burned and cannibalized have been

found in various ruins dated around 800 A.D. One human scalp was found with the hair still carefully done up. Was the scalp brought back by a raiding party so the proper ceremonies could be held to prevent the spirit of the killed person from exacting vengeance?

As horrible as all this seems, the Anasazi have always been viewed by archaeologists as gentle, farming people. Their lifeways involved an enormous amount of hard work. But there was also time for the ceremonies and rituals that were connected to all aspects of their lives. There was time to ponder the mystery of life. What was a typical day in the life of an Anasazi who lived in Mesa Verde or Chaco Canyon and belonged to a huge network of other towns and people?

An example of the outstanding stonework that the Anasazi are so famous for. It surpasses the finest stonework done in Europe at the time (1100 A.D.) Where did they learn this skill?

(Courtesy of Chaco Culture National Historic Park, National Park Service.)

The Anasazi in the Year 1050 A.D.

There were three main centers of Anasazi life in the Southwest: the Mesa Verde area in southwestern Colorado, the Chaco Canyon area in northwestern New Mexico, and the Kayenta area in northeastern Arizona. The ancient ruins most associated with the western Kayenta area are Betatakin and Kiet Siel located in Navajo National Monument.

Those who lived in Chaco Canyon reached a higher level of architectural development than any of their neighbors. Pueblo Bonito contains over 800 rooms and kivas! The Chacoans were at their peak two hundred years before the cliff dwellings of Mesa Verde and Kayenta were built and construction ceased in Chaco Canyon in 1132 A.D. Other eastern

Anasazi ruins are Aztec, Bandelier, and Pecos National Monuments, all in New Mexico.

The inhabitants of Mesa Verde lived in aboveground structures until after about 1150 or 1200 A.D. when they began moving into the cliff dwellings. They stayed at Mesa Verde long after the citizens of Chaco Canyon had left their own pueblos. When the Mesa Verdans left, they scattered in all directions. Some may have gone to Chaco Canyon, which was only a two-day walk. Others may have joined the Anasazi who were making their way to the Hopi mesas of today. Still others joined kin in the Rio Grande area. All became the Pueblos of today.

In thinking about what life was like for the Anasazi before they left their early settlements, it is important to remember that the difference in living in the biggest town, Pueblo Bonito in Chaco Canyon, and the small dwellings of Mesa Verde would be like comparing living in New York City today to living in a small town in New England. Chaco Canyon had a more exotic flavor with traders flowing in from Mexico and California with unusual shells and colorful birds. The people of Mesa Verde and the Kayenta area, on the other hand, had a spectacular view from their cliff houses. The architectural styles of the cliff dwellers and large towns in Chaco Canyon were different, but in the outlying areas they were more similar. The Chacoans lived quite simply in one-family dwellings that contained a living room, sleeping

quarters, and a kiva. The larger towns of Chaco Canyon stand out as being much more sophisticated in design and stonework than those of their neighbors. There may have been as many as fifteen thousand people living in that one area. That is one reason archaeologists speculate that perhaps cities such as Pueblo Bonito in Chaco Canyon were a central place where everyone came for ceremonies, trading, community, or for food which had been stored there. Scientists wonder, was there an elite class living at Chaco?

Overall, though, the people who used to inhabit the many ruins scattered all over the Southwest had much in common. Everyone, for example, had to contribute for survival. There were many mouths to feed. It didn't rain often in the desert country, but when the skies began to darken, everyone ran to help collect water. When the weather cooperated and there was enough rain, all went smoothly.

At pueblos all over the Southwest, everyone awoke with the sun. All the colors of the rainbow were displayed at sunrise. The Southwest is known for the colors of the sky during sunrise and sunset. The rooms were small and dark, and families were crowded. Each family had a room for storage and one that served for eating, sleeping, and living. When possible, the people stayed outdoors. Most of the cooking was done in the plaza, which was in many cases the roof of the kiva. There were no stairways;

everyone scrambled up and down ladders to reach their rooms. There was very little privacy. Because there were no hallways, everyone marched through each other's rooms to get to their own.

A child would have a breakfast of corn gruel with maybe a few seeds thrown in. Younger children stayed with their mothers, but in summer, the older children would head out to the fields to plant corn, squash, and beans.

Some of the women met at a special room where they would grind corn all day. They used sandstone slabs as their grinding stones. These were given the name *metate* by the Spanish. They ground the corn against the metate with a smaller stone called a *mano* (Spanish for "hand"). Most of the people wore their teeth down by the time they were forty as sand would rub off into the corn. Sitting hunched over the sandstone slab grinding all day was hard work. It made the women old before their time.

While the women ground the corn, one of the men would sit in the door playing a wooden flute. The women would move the stones to the music and sing together. There was much ceremony around their main crop, corn. Corn was believed to have a spirit, just as everything else did. It gave the Anasazi life.

After breakfast, the masons would begin shaping stones and other artisans would begin pounding leather or making tools. Some of the men would head out to find timber to make beams. It wasn't unusual for them to go many miles for wood and then to drag it back. Others left early with bows and arrows to hunt deer, mountain sheep, rabbits, and birds. At first, the Anasazi imported their cotton from the Mogollon people, but later they grew their own.

Traders came with their wares including the colorful birds, macaws, that the Anasazi liked so well. Copper was another favorite import. Other traders would arrive with shells from California. The Anasazi traded their turquoise and pottery in return for these items.

The Anasazi were smaller than the people of today. The men were only about 5′3″ and the women were shorter. Everyone wore jewelry. Necklaces, pendants, bracelets, and rings were popular. They didn't wear many clothes, especially in the hot months. All wore sandals. In the winter, they wore hide cloaks and fur blankets. The men wore their hair long and braided. Women's hairdos were done up in fancy styles.

Children were surely cherished. Many died in infancy and early childhood, usually stemming from an improperly balanced diet. Pneumonia was another common cause of death. Conditions were not very sanitary and diseases developed as a result, as they do today. The adults were lucky to live to the age of forty, which seems very young today.

Babies had their own special fur blankets. Infants were tied snugly to boards that were attached to their mothers' backs. At about the time of puberty, children were initiated into the mysteries of religion and marriage. It is common to find pictographs of those ceremonies on walls of caves or kivas.

Anasazi society was matrilocal, where all the women in a village are closely related. The house and all the furnishings belonged to the woman. She and her sisters, aunts, and grandmother formed the stable family unit. The men were responsible for religious activities which took place in the kivas.

Out on the plaza, women made pottery. Their pottery was famous even in those days. The Anasazi women dreamed their pottery. The images that appeared in their dreams found their way onto the various pots. To them it wasn't just repeating one pattern over and over. The images and swirls never seemed the same. Many miniature pots have been found at various ruins, suggesting that the children learned to make pottery when young. It was easy to tell which style of pottery belonged to a particular group of people.

One could spend a lifetime studying Anasazi pottery. The process of making pottery has changed little since the time of the Anasazi. The clay is ground up so that it won't be lumpy. It is moistened and some form of temper is added to keep the pot from cracking while drying and firing. Some tempers are sand, crushed rock, and ground potsherds. All their wares were built up and shaped by hand. The potter's wheel did not exist. The potter shaped coils of clay and constructed the walls of the jar by overlapping the coils. Decorations were added. After drying, the pots were fired. This was done in Anasazi times by covering them with wood and setting the wood on fire.

Most of the Anasazi pots were made with round, rather than flat, bottoms. The flat bottoms weren't necessary because they didn't set the pots on tables.

It is generally believed that pottery-making began in Mesoamerica and the Anasazi learned about it from traders. It didn't take long, however, for the Anasazi to develop their own styles. The earliest pottery was plain grey and unpolished. It is obvious from the pots and potsherds that have been found that they experimented quite a lot with shapes and sizes. Then they began adding paints. In the Kayenta area, paint was made from plant juices. In other areas, the paints were minerals, usually iron which turns black in the process. The iron paint turned red when the pots were oxidized.

They made jars, bowls of every description, dippers, mugs, pitchers, and canteens. The designs and shapes varied from one region to the next. The Kayenta black-on-white style is one of the best-known today. The people in Mesa Verde imported pots from the Kayenta people. Some of the most outstanding pottery was made between 1100 and 1300. By the 1300s, potters were making new shapes, new color combinations and the containers were thicker.

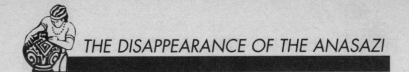

Black-on-white pottery generally died out and was replaced by black-on-yellow and multicolored pottery in the Hopi area.

Today the Anasazi Pueblo pottery tradition is stronger than ever.

The only domestic animals were turkeys and dogs. Dogs were useful as guards and were a source of soft fur. The turkeys were mostly used for their feathers, but the meat was eaten sometimes. It was fun for the young children to chase the turkeys around the plaza. When they tired of that, they'd chase each other.

There were games, too. Bone dice have been found in the ruins. The Hohokam introduced a game that was a cross between basketball and soccer. It originally started with the Mayas. The idea was to pass a solid ball of rubber through hoops mounted at the ends of an arena. The players could not touch the ball with their hands. They had to knock or butt the ball through the goal.

At night, an elder would go out to watch the sunset. The men and their sons would gather in the kivas by the firelight and tell stories. The storytelling was much more than entertainment. The storyteller would tell their myth of creation. They believed that the telling helped to save the world from death and destruction. The word was power. It could cure or heal or ward off evil.

Many ceremonies were planned around the growing season. Anasazi life was closely bound to land and water. A good deal of energy was used to assure an adequate supply of both. By concentrating his or her thoughts on the corn plant, for example, a Hopi feels he or she can influence its growth. These people hoped they could affect the rest of the universe—make it rain, for example. Was this belief passed down from the Anasazi?

All went well for hundreds of years for the Anasazi. The period between 700 and 1100 A.D. had been a time of learning and incredible development. These ancient people had created a civilization that would amaze archaeologists who would try to solve the mystery of their disappearance centuries later. The Anasazi must have been puzzled when trouble came. And trouble did come. The question is, what was powerful enough to make them leave? They had suffered periods of drought before, but had always gotten through the crisis. There had been incidents over the years of wandering nomads attacking, but nothing that drove the Anasazi off.

It is evident from some of the late buildings, both at Chaco Canyon and at Mesa Verde, that trouble was afoot. During the thirteenth century, the Anasazi were choosing locations that were easier to defend. They moved their homes into almost inaccessible caves and other places difficult to reach. They began adding defensive walls. Who was attacking? Chaco Canyon was abandoned before the people

of Mesa Verde even considered leaving. As early as 1132 many Chacoans had left the region. By 1300 all the original caves, cliff houses, and desert homes were abandoned.

Two archaeologists climbed cliffs in the Kayenta Valley and found ruins that dated back to between 1250 and 1300. They were struck by the depth of fear the people living there must have experienced. They felt sure they had moved up into the cliffs to get away from raiders. They found skeletons with no skulls, skulls with foreheads bashed in, and signs of fire in those sites in the open. The Anasazi had lived peaceful lives for centuries. Why the violence?

It seems the Anasazi wanted to hang on. The people at Mesa Verde built Sun Temple, a labyrinth-type building way out on a mesa. It was meant to enclose the worshiper. It would also carry his or her eye out above the earth so that he or she was lifted to the clouds.

Alfonso Ortiz of the Tewa clan said, "I believe the Sun Temple represents a last great effort. . . to read the heavens, to [understand] the reason for the ordeal." The people were trying to appease the gods by building a special place of worship in their honor. Prayers and ceremonies had always brought rain eventually. What was happening this time?

What was the ordeal? Enemies? Drought? Had too many people come together in one place where there was no real leadership?

THE ANASAZI IN THE YEAR 1050 A.D.

A Hopi legend says the Hopi were the builders of the Chaco pueblos. To keep the valley fertile, they held races every year. A priest carrying a jar of sacred water would run through the canyon and the fastest men of each clan would try to catch him. The sacred water would bring rain to the fields of the clan that caught him. As the canyon became more and more populated, the annual races lost their sacred character. They became mere sporting events. Because of this, rain became scarce. The elders of the clans came together and said they must leave. It was their punishment for allowing the games to be corrupted. One clan went to Canyon de Chelly and another built the cliff houses in Kayenta. Eventually they were reunited on the mesas they now occupy in eastern Arizona.

Some call the next period in the lives of the Anasazi a regressive period, which means to go backward. Others see it as a time of further development. No matter how it is viewed, it began a new chapter in the history of a people who had arrived in the Southwest more than a thousand years before.

It is sad to think of the mass migration of the Anasazi out of the fantastic civilization they had created. Perhaps that is because we know the history of bloodshed that lay ahead of them. What different fate would they have experienced had they stayed in the Four Corners area? Why did they leave?

Abandonment!

A Hopi migration myth tells that the Hopi are in their Fourth World after having gone through three worlds. There would be four migrations required of the Hopis in this world. Masaw, the guardian spirit of the Fourth World, instructed the people about how they were to make the migrations, how they were to recognize their new home, and how they were to live once they got there. Masaw gave a small water jar to each clan. One person from the clan would be selected to carry the jar. At each migration the jar would be planted again. As long as they had the jar, there would be water.

The migrations were meant to purify the people, getting rid of all the evil from the past worlds. By traveling to all the farthest corners of the land during their four migrations, these chosen people finally came to settle on the vast dry plateau that stretches

Fajada Butte from a distance. This is the site of the famed "Sun Dagger Clock" which, like Stonehenge in England, marks the summer solstice, or longest day of the year.

(Courtesy of Chaco Culture National Historic Park, National Park Service.)

between the Colorado and Rio Grande Rivers. This is where they are today.

By 1300 A.D. the canyons, the cliff dwellings, the vast structures at Chaco Canyon stood silent in the sun. The sun made its marks on the stone, marking the solstices and equinoxes, but no one was there to report it. Some of the cliff houses had only been lived in for a few generations. The overriding mystery concerning the Anasazi is why they left. In the early part of this century, stories went around about the "lost cities" whose inhabitants had mysteriously vanished, leaving no traces.

There is no question in the minds of archaeologists that the Anasazi were losing a battle with a difficult environment. Though experts deny that all the Anasazi left at once, it does seem like a mass exodus when considering the hundreds of years it took them to settle in the Southwest.

A drought that occurred between the years of 1276 and 1299 played a major role in the people's leaving. Two or three years of crop failure would bring famine. With the population explosion that had been going on, there were too many mouths to feed. The lack of food surely produced tension among the Anasazi.

But what about Chaco Canyon, which had already emptied out before the drought? The first thought that comes to mind is defense. There isn't much evidence to support this; however, it is curious that at Chaco only one door in that huge complex of rooms opens to the outside. And why did they start burying their dead beneath the floors of their houses? Was it to protect the dead from invaders, too? Or were they afraid to go out to bury their dead?

The Chacoans needed construction materials and firewood, and these were getting harder to find. There were no environmental groups issuing warnings to the Anasazi as they do today. As closely connected to the land as they were, they were causing damage to the earth. It has been estimated that over 5,000 trees were used to build one settlement in Chaco Canyon. This speeded up the recession of the pine forest and soil erosion. With the trees gone, there was no root system to slow the rush of flood waters in wet years.

The cutting of *arroyos*, or gullies, which was

caused by a change in rainfall pattern, was given as the chief cause of abandonment by one archaeologist. Summer storms in the Southwest are violent and destructive. Thousands of gallons of water can be collected from one storm. However, most of the water, instead of being soaked up by the ground, runs off to the nearest drainage. It carries a lot of soil with it and at the same time carves gullies as it goes. Increasing cold was another problem that developed for the Anasazi, which meant that more wood must be burned to keep the plants protected from frost.

Some scientists have speculated that a new disease infected the population such as smallpox or influenza, but there isn't much evidence to support that theory.

As life became more difficult for the Anasazi, there were probably more disruptions among clans and villages. Maybe some people left to escape the bickering. A notion popular among some anthropologists is that the great towns grew too large. The Anasazi had managed to maintain their separate family units in a democratic atmosphere, but as the population grew, it would have been more difficult. The Pueblo people may have chosen to stick with democracy and small towns.

Another theory is the migration theory. Archaeologists have studied patterns of abandonment that have occurred throughout the world. They point out that abandonment of villages, towns, and cities was

not uncommon in most of the pre-Columbian Western Hemisphere. Thousands of sites, from Mexico to huge Mississippi Valley settlements, had been abandoned before the Europeans ventured into America. Abandoning small areas one or more times was not an uncommon Anasazi pattern.

The religious system could have caused major changes, particularly at Chaco Canyon where the Mexican influence seemed to be growing stronger. Did the presence of the Great Kivas indicate there was a religious cult that had entered the Anasazi domain? Perhaps the people turned to the priests to help them with their new problems. When the priests obviously couldn't help, the people might have lost faith in the priests altogether. At this point, they may have departed in search of places more favored by the gods.

The movement outward was steady. The settlement in New Mexico called Aztec that was founded in 1100 A.D. was abandoned for the second time around 1300. The people there made a quick departure. They sealed all their doors and windows. Did they plan to return some day and wanted to protect the things they left behind?

For a long time, the Navajo were blamed for driving the Anasazi out during this period, but they didn't arrive in the Southwest until the 1500s. Albert Laughter, a Navajo, explained how he felt a kinship to the vanished ones. He added, "My grandmother

A close-up of the kiva at Pueblo Bonito.
(Courtesy of Chaco Culture National Historic Park, National Park Service.)

says the Anasazi became over-confident and ignored the gods. They went too far and were punished."

Another Navajo elder agreed. "They disobeyed nature. The gods sent hurricanes and lightning and drove them away."

Where did they go? Archaeologist Linda Cordell believes the abandonments were gradual. She imagines the younger people left first, seeking a better life in new villages. They no doubt heard of the new villages from traders. They went to the villages founded along the northern Rio Grande tributaries, to the Hopi mesas, to the area called the Upper Little Colorado River drainage and the Zuni Plateau. One group of Anasazi went to the Flagstaff, Arizona, area after 1064. A volcano erupted, causing them to move south where they joined tribes of Hohokam, who had a similar culture. On the plateau were the Sinagua (their name is Spanish for "without water") who were also farmers. Soon all migrated back to the volcano area: Sinagua, Anasazi, and Hohokam together. The Sinagua and Hohokam absorbed the Anasazi culture, which is evident from the building styles. They built the Casa Grande settlement, finishing it around 1300.

The builders of Betatakin and Kiet Siel and other cliff houses moved fifty or sixty miles to Antelope Mesa and Black Mesa, becoming the Hopi of today. The Hopi today occupy three mesas about 600 feet high that are on Black Mesa. The first Hopi arrived here about 1150. Their migration myth is their claim to the land.

Many new settlements were founded, or joined, by the Anasazi. The Homolovi ruins and Chavez Pass are ancestral Hopi sites. Atsinna is one of the ancestral Zuni towns, and Puye is one of the ancestral villages of the modern Pueblo people of Santa Clara on the Rio Grande. Around 1300 A.D. three families moved into an area above a spring and founded Arroyo Hondo in New Mexico. Within thirty years the population had grown to 1,500. These people continued their farming. They began painting murals on kiva walls that portrayed ritual themes of the supernatural world. They became the modern Keresan population.

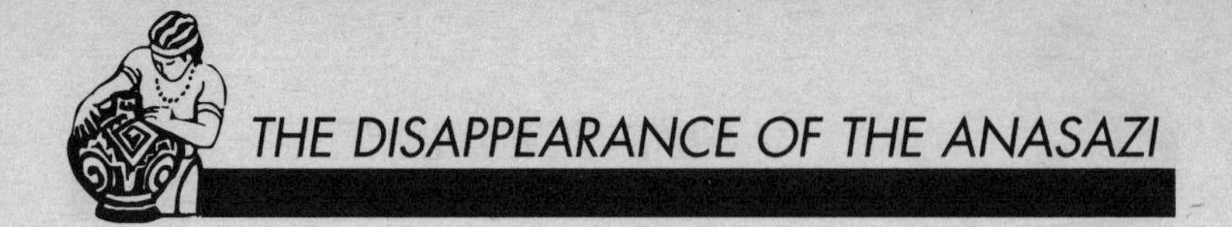

The descendants of the ancient Anasazi world were a growing and active group at the turn of the sixteenth century. It was during this period that the *kachinas*, or spirit gods, became a major part of the new Pueblo culture. The cult of the kachinas came from Mexico. The Hopi and Zuni believe that many years ago in a time of famine supernatural beings called kachinas came to them from the distant mountains. They brought food and saved many lives. They are an important part of the ceremonies held today.

Today's Zuni and Hopi are more isolated than the rest of their Pueblo kin. They tend to accept all events as being the will of the Creator. They also share the myth of the kachinas. The Rio Grande people, or the easternmost Pueblo, became tougher because they were more exposed to the warlike tribes that started coming in the 1500s such as the Ute, the Navajo, and the Comanche.

Another part of the mystery of the Anasazi is why they did not seem to try to recreate their fantastic towns in the new places where they settled. Why didn't they concentrate in one great cultural center like Chaco Canyon or create a large civilization such as the one the Aztecs had built in Mexico?

Pueblo leaders are interchangeable. No one person is in charge. The Hopi cling to their clan tradition. It is not uncommon for one clan to be unaware of the practices of another clan. Each village has its own

rituals and each kiva fraternity has its own secret rites that are not shared with any other group. The Hopi are ruled by their religion, not by politics. If there was a strong government at Chaco Canyon, the Anasazi who lived there did not carry it with them. Neither did they carry the late tradition of the Tri-Walls and the Sun Temple at Mesa Verde. They didn't take their knowledge about roads or irrigation systems, both of which require strong leadership to build and maintain. Archaeologist Linda Cordell believes that when the system collapsed, the Anasazi were unable to return to the high level of energy necessary to re-establish it.

All the troubles that caused the Anasazi to leave, however, seem almost minor in light of what was to come. The Navajo and other nomadic tribes moved into the area in the 1500s. In 1540 the Spaniards invaded. Their goal was to destroy the religion of the "savages" and replace it with their own. They were followed by the Americans in the mid-1800s who brought their own brand of religion, along with sugar, alcohol, and disease. The result is one of the saddest chapters in American history.

The Anasazi Today

The Hopi have sacred tablets that tell of their beginnings, their migrations in the wilderness, and the white man who will come and bring wisdom and love. It tells them they are the chosen ones, much like the Israelites are called "the chosen ones" in the Bible. These teachings are as meaningful to them as the teachings of the Bible are to Christians and Jews and as the teachings of the Koranau to Moslem. One of the Hopi legends is called "The Legend of the Bahana." Bahana is the white brother or white savior of the Hopi. The legend is very similar to an ancient legend of the Mayas and Toltecs in Mexico. Bahana came up with the people from the underworld and was said to have great wisdom. He set out on a journey to the rising sun, promising to return with many benefits for the people. The Hopi believe that when he comes there will be no more fighting and trouble.

It was this legend that led the Hopi people to allow the Spanish priests into their country. The people thought that at last the Bahana had come. They had never seen a white man, nor had they ever seen a horse or guns.

At first the newcomers were consumed by their search for gold and their desire to convert all heathens to their religion, Christianity. The first Spaniards arrived in small groups of soldiers and priests, but they brought with them their servants. They took food and other provisions from the Pueblos and if the Pueblos refused, they were severely punished. The Spaniards were surprised to find the Pueblos were so civilized. A Spanish soldier wrote, "They do not have chiefs as in New Spain, but are ruled by a council of the oldest men. They have priests who preach to them who are called Papas. These are the elders. . . . They tell them how to live." But it was upsetting to the Spaniards to find that these humans had reached a similar level of achievement as they, and in some cases a higher moral and spiritual level.

It wasn't long before the people whose name Hopi means "Peaceful Ones" were terrified of the Spaniards. They felt the Spanish would as soon kill them as look at them. The Spaniards had already conquered Peru and Mexico. The Pueblos gave in to many of their demands. But the one area where they would not bend was their religion. The Spanish priests became the Pueblos biggest enemies, moving into their communities, abusing their children, and treating the Native Americans as though they were slaves, forcing them to farm and mine and serve the Spanish invaders. The Spanish betrayed their own religion by the way they acted. Many Spaniards believed that the Indians were savages, less than human and therefore did not have to be treated like humans. The Pueblos finally rose up and attacked, driving the Spaniards out for about ten years.

The Spaniards tried three more times to retake the Pueblo area—in 1681, in 1688, and in 1689 but were unsuccessful. In 1692 and 1693 they finally succeeded. The Hopi, however, resisted the reconquest and were never again under Spanish domination.

If the Spanish weren't problem enough, wandering nomads were again making life difficult. Years earlier, one theory goes, invading nomads drove the Anasazi away from their homes. Now, around 1600, their descendants, the modern Pueblo, were overrun again by a people who called themselves Dine. The word *dine* means "the People," but the Hopi Pueblo people called them *apachu*, meaning "stranger" or "enemy." The Spanish mispronounced this term as Apache. They also gave the Dine their own name, Navajo.

The new tribes came from Alaska and Canada. They were not farmers. They traveled in small bands and raided the fields the Pueblo people had planted.

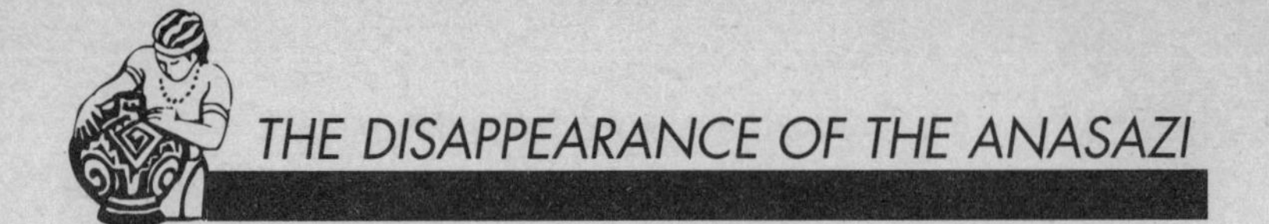

They didn't want to settle down in small towns the way the Pueblo had.

The Pueblo tried to fight back, but they were already exhausted by their long, hopeless struggle with the Spanish. The Pueblos hated war. If they took life, they had to be purified in special ceremonies when they returned. The Apache/Navajo made life miserable for the Pueblo people through the first half of the nineteenth century. In the old days, their ancestors, the Anasazi, would have migrated. But now that the Spanish ruled them, they were not allowed to move. Besides, the Spanish now owned all the best land.

Along with strife, the Europeans had brought terrible diseases to which the Pueblo had no resistance. Many died from smallpox and other sicknesses. In fact, epidemics cut the populations of most tribes in half.

The Navajo and Apache were also raiding the new breed of whites coming to the Southwest. By 1822 Mexico had won independence from the Spanish and the Native Americans had new rulers. But Mexican rule didn't last long. The United States was expanding. In 1846 U.S. President Polk declared war against Mexico. The Americans went in and took what they wanted, but there was no bloodshed. Mexico gave up New Mexico, Arizona, Utah, Nevada, and California to the United States.

The descendants of the Anasazi were now to be

under the control of the Bureau of Indian Affairs, part of the United States government. After a long and devastating war, the Apaches and Navajo also fell under the laws of the United States. The Pueblos at this point were relieved that at least they wouldn't be attacked any longer by the tribes. They hoped once again that these white people would treat them kindly and allow them their own lifeways. Maybe Bahana was among the white man?

But this was not to be. The Americans did not apply their freedom ideals to the conquered "savages": there was to be no freedom of religion. They hated the religion of the Native Americans. They thought it primitive. In their racial prejudice against peoples with darker skin, they did not see the Indians as human beings. They were afraid of them and their world of spirits and supernatural beings. Frank Waters, a writer who spent a great deal of time with the Hopis, wrote, in 1963, "It's hard to say why they seem so strange to us. Their songs and dance form rhythmical patterns. The costumes and decorations are even more simple. Have we grown so far away from our earth that we read no meaning in the elements of its mineral, plant and animal kingdom?"

The conquering Americans showed no respect for the traditions or lifeways of those people already living there. Their children were taken away to special Indian schools, sometimes hundreds of miles away, so they could learn the American way. Although

these children learned to read and write and to speak English they learned sad things as well. The Native American children learned about loss. They learned prejudice. They learned that their parents' ways were not acceptable in the big world away from the mesas and the kachinas. Today, part of this is expressed in some sad statistics. Native American infants today die much more frequently, and the adults die younger, than the rest of Americans. There are many more suicides among the young than anywhere else in the country. The introduction of alcohol and sugar to the Native Americans has probably caused more devastation than ten thousand soldiers could have done. Today there is a high rate of alcoholism among the Native Americans.

The stresses from without gave birth to stresses within. The Hopis fought bitterly among themselves. Some people blame the new religion, Christianity, for dividing brother against brother. The inhabitants of one village attacked another village when it began adopting the white religion. There are those today who cling to the traditional ways learned from the Anasazi and others who want to progress and adapt to the modern world.

The Hopis, more than any other descendants of the Anasazi, have managed to remain aloof from the rest of the world. In a symbolic way, it is as though they boarded a spaceship a long time ago and were swept to the high mesas they now inhabit. They remain

A staircase carved into the side of a cliff at Chaco Canyon by the Anasazi. Today it is called the Jackson Staircase in honor of the white man who rediscovered it, William Henry Jackson.

(Courtesy of Chaco Culture National Historic Park, National Park Service.)

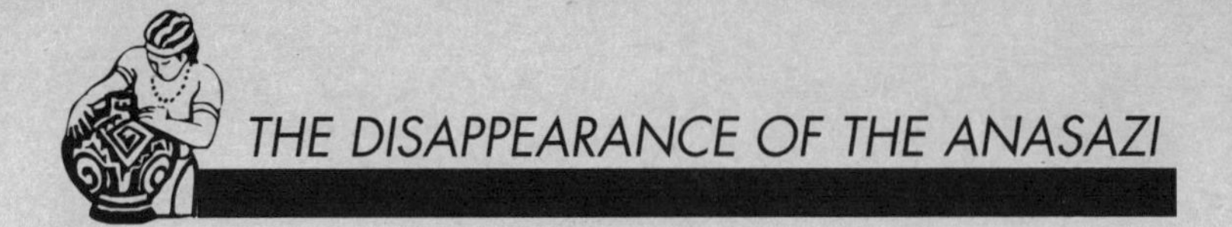

wary of the whites. Outsiders are not welcome in Hopi mesas.

They have proven their ability to survive over the millennia. It would be easy to idealize the Hopi, but that wouldn't be fair. They are in a period of transition now. Change is slowly occurring in the attitudes of the whites and the Native Americans. The elders have begun to tell their stories before they are lost forever. Television gives their children a view of the world away from the mesas, and some are choosing to follow it. The Pueblos face the problem today of absorbing American technology and ways without losing their communal identity. They will have to find a way to balance their old lifeways with the new.

Some people feel that the time of the Anasazi was so long ago that they are mostly forgotten by their descendants today. That is hard to believe. The mystery of the Anasazi comes alive in the ceremonies and rituals of the Pueblos that are performed every year. Visitors say the ceremonies take them back before time, before memory. The Anasazi live in the stories told deep down in the kivas, in the drums that beat through the night, and in the dreams of the women who mold pottery and the men who weave cotton down below.

The attitude of whites is changing. The old textbooks that glorify conquering of the Indians are slowly being replaced with books that focus on what really happened.

THE ANASAZI TODAY

Many people today are seeking out the Native American ways. With all the talk of diminishing rain forests, holes in the atmosphere from pollution, and nuclear wastes, to name but a few of the problems affecting the Earth today, there is more emphasis on developing communion with the land. What better teachers are there than the Native Americans? Books are being written by white people on their experiences with Native American teachers. It is not uncommon to find whites in the Northeast creating a Native American weekend, where they dress in their costumes and chant their songs. Healing ceremonies have become popular with many people—not only Indians. A psychoanalytic group in Connecticut combines the teachings of Native Americans with those of the founders of Western psychology.

Modern people are afraid to face the emptiness of each individual's world. But to the Native American there was no such thing as emptiness in the world. Every object around him or her was alive with spirit. Margot Astrov wrote, "The earth and tree and stone and the wide scope of the heaven were [inhabited] by numberless supernaturals and the wandering souls of the dead."

What is going on between the Native Americans and the U.S. government and big business is still frightening. Thomas Banyacya, Sr., a Hopi elder, speaks frankly about the way the U.S. government divided up Native American land in 1972. It is called

the "joint-use" area, meaning it is to be shared by various tribes. Banyacya and three other men were appointed by the elders of the Hopi Third Mesa to tell the outside world of the warnings contained in the Hopi prophecies. Much has been written about the clashes between the Hopis and the Navajo over the land that they are forced to use together. The conflict is over Big Mountain, an area that Banyacya's son calls the Hopi Jerusalem. It also has big deposits of coal, uranium, and oil shale. The uranium, of course, would be used to make bombs. Some White businesses want to drive the Native Americans off the land so they can have what's under it, according to Banyacya.

He also said, "The Navajos help guard the land for the Hopi. This is their sacred land too. The White Man is the one who needs to leave before Nature intervenes. The Great Spirit made us caretakers of this land. We take care of it with our prayers and our ceremony. Now you poison it!"

Thomas Berry, a well-known historian who writes about the Earth, wrote, "The fate of the continent [North America], the fate of the Indian, and our own fate are finally identical. None can be saved except in and through the others."

Where did they come from and where did they go has been the overriding mystery around the Anasazi for centuries. Scientists have devoted a great deal of

time, money, and effort to solving those concrete mysteries. However, the case is never closed. There is always one more finding, one more clue. Where did they come from? Were they connected to other societies all over the world? Did their trading occur further south than Mexico? Did some of their ideas come from as far away as Peru and the fabulous Inca civilization? Or did the Anasazi civilization just spring up on its own, the people developing their technology and religion as they went? There is as yet no complete answer.

In 1991, an article appeared in the *Washington Post* saying that scientists offered new evidence that all living humans share a single African ancestor—a woman who lived about 200,000 years ago. They claim her descendants swept across the Earth, replacing a more primitive human species as they went. Statements such as these boggle the imagination. Perhaps one day all will see the inhabitants of the world as one human family like the Anasazi did before the days of the invaders.

The Hopi say the emergence to the Fifth World has begun. It is being made by the humble people of little nations, tribes, and racial minorities. "You can read this in the earth itself," they say. "Plant forms from previous worlds are beginning to spring up as seeds. This could start a new study of botany if people were wise enough to read them. The same kinds of seeds are being planted in the sky as stars. The same kind

of seeds are being planted in our hearts. All these are the same, depending how you look at them."

Just like William Henry Jackson sensed when he first entered "Two-Story Cliff House" in 1874, people today feel that eyes are watching them when they visit the land of the Anasazi. They feel their presence. They are there. It is no doubt those are presences who hold the knowledge of the beginning of the Anasazi and of their abandonment of their homes. And maybe even to the beginning and end of our world as we know it.

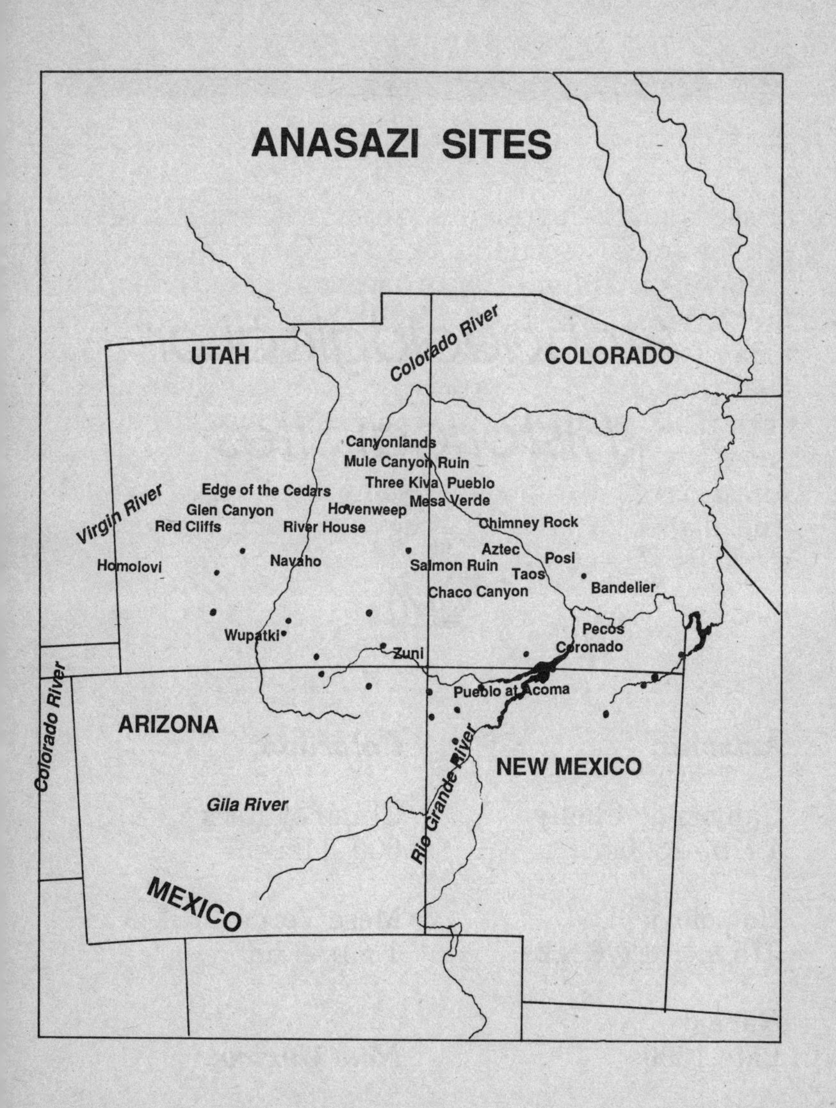

ANASAZI SITES
UTAH
COLORADO
Colorado River
Canyonlands
Mule Canyon Ruin
Three Kiva Pueblo
Mesa Verde
Edge of the Cedars
Hovenweep
Glen Canyon
Red Cliffs
River House
Virgin River
Chimney Rock
Aztec
Posi
Homolovi
Navaho
Salmon Ruin
Taos
Bandelier
Chaco Canyon
Wupatki
Pecos
Coronado
Zuni
Colorado River
Pueblo at Acoma
ARIZONA
NEW MEXICO
Rio Grande River
Gila River
MEXICO

Archaeological or Historical Sites

***Arizona*:**

Canyon de Chelly
1 A.D.–1300s

Homolovi
375 B.C.–1276 A.D.

Navajo
Late 1200s

Wupatki
1100–1225

***Colorado*:**

Chimney Rock
600–1150

Mesa Verde
1 A.D.–1300

***New Mexico*:**

Aztec
1100–1300

Bandelier
1100–1525 A.D.

Chaco Canyon
200 B.C.–1200

Coronado
1325–1549

Pecos
1150–1450

Posi
1300s–1400s

Pueblo of Acoma
1100–present

Salmon Ruin
1150–1300 A.D.

Taos
900–present

Zuni
900–present

Utah:

Canyonlands
800 A.D.–1250

Edge of the Cedars
700 A.D.–1200 A.D.

Glen Canyon
180 A.D.–1300 A.D.

Hovenweep
1050–1300

Mule Canyon Ruin
1100–1200

Red Cliffs
1100–1200

River House
1100–1200

Three Kiva Pueblo
1100–1200

Native American Museums in Anasazi Territory

***Arizona*:**

Arizona State Museum
University of Arizona
Tucson

Heard Museum
Phoenix

Museum of Northern Arizona
Flagstaff

Pueblo Grande Museum
Phoenix

***Colorado*:**

Denver Art Museum
Denver

Denver Museum of Natural History
Denver

Ute Indian Museum

***New Mexico*:**

Indian Pueblo Cultural Center
Albuquerque

Institute of American Indian Arts
Santa Fe

Maxwell Museum of Anthropology
Albuquerque

Mescalero Apache Cultural Center
Mescalero

Museum of Indian Arts and Culture
Santa Fe

Taos Pueblo
Taos

Western New Mexico University Museum
Silver City

Zuni Pueblo
Zuni

Utah:

College of Eastern Utah Prehistoric Museum
Price

Utah Museum of Natural History
Salt Lake City

Washington, D.C.:

National Museum of Natural History
Smithsonian Institution
District of Columbia

Bibliography

Ambler, Richard. *The Anasazi*. Flagstaff, Arizona: Museum of Northern Arizona, 1989.

Anderson, Douglas and Barbara. *Chaco Canyon*. Globe, Arizona: Southwest Parks and Monuments Association, 1976.

Astrov, Margot. *American Indian Prose and Poetry*. New York: Capricorn Books, 1962.

Beckley, Timothy Green. *The American Indian UFO—Starseed Connection*. New Brunswick, New Jersey: Inner Light Publications, 1992.

Berry, Thomas. *The Dream of the Earth*. San Francisco: Sierra Club Books, 1988.

Calvin, William H. *The River that Flows Uphill*. New York: Macmillan Publishing Company, 1986.

Canby, Thomas Y. "Riddles in the Ruins." *National Geographic*, November 1982, pp. 554-592.

BIBLIOGRAPHY

Copper, Philip and the editors of Smithsonian Books. *The Smithsonian Book of North American Indians*. Washington, DC: Smithsonian Books, 1986.

Creamer, Winifred and Jonathan Haas. "Pueblo: Search for the Ancient Ones." *National Geographic*, October 1991, pp. 84-99.

Doolittle, Jerome and the editors of Time-Life Books. *Canyons and Mesas*. New York: Time Inc., 1974.

Editors of *American Heritage*. *The American Heritage Book of Indians*. New York: American Heritage/Bonanza Books, 1961.

Jones, Dewitt and Linda S. Cordell. *Anasazi World*. Portland, Oregon: Graphic Arts Center Publishing Company, 1985.

Laskin, David. "New Mexico's Mysterious Anasazi Ruins." *The New York Times*, September 22, 1991.

Michell, John. *Secrets of the Stones*. Rochester, Vermont: Inner Traditions, 1989.

Nequatewa, Edmund. *Truth of a Hopi*. Flagstaff, Arizona: Museum of Northern Arizona, 1967.

Otiz, Alfonso. "Origins: Through Tewa Eyes." *National Geographic*, October 1991, pp. 6-13.

Reader's Digest. *Mysteries of the Ancient Americas*. Pleasantville, New York: Reader's Digest Association, Inc., 1986.

Scully, Vincent. *Pueblo/Mountain, Village, Dance*.

New York: The Viking Press, 1975.

Silverberg, Robert. *The Old Ones, Indians of the American Southwest.* New York: New York Graphic Society Publishers, Ltd., 1965.

Sturtevant, William C. and Alfonso Ortiz, eds. *Handbook of the North American Indians Southwest, Vol. 9.* Washington, DC: Smithsonian Institution, 1979.

Wall, Steve and Harvey Arden. *Wisdomkeepers, Meetings with Native American Spiritual Elders.* Hillsboro, Oregon: Beyond Words Publishing, 1990.

Waters, Frank. *Book of the Hopi.* New York: The Viking Press, 1963.

Weaver, Donald E., Jr. *Images on Stone.* Flagstaff, Arizona: The Museum of Northern Arizona, 1984.

Wenger, Gilbert R. *The Story of Mesa Verde National Park.* Mesa Verde, Colorado: Mesa Verde Museum Association, Inc., 1980.